W9-AHN-730

Secret Agents

by Paul Thomas

Thameside Press

Distributed in the United States by
Smart Apple Media
1980 Lookout Drive
North Mankato, MN 56003

Text copyright © Paul Thomas

ISBN 1-931983-42-9

Library of Congress Control Number 2002 141368

Printed by Midas, Hong Kong

Editor: Christine Hatt
Series designer: Hayley Cove
Picture researcher: Diana Morris
Consultant: Hazel Mary Martell

J
327.12
THO

Photographic credits
AKG, London:11(top), 24(top), 30, 31(bottom), 32(top), 33, 36(bottom), 43(top), 43(bottom). Bridgeman Art
Library: 7(bottom) British Library; 12 Private Collection; 14 Anne Brown Military Academy, Providence, R.I.;
23(top) The Fine Art Society, London; 23(bottom) Christies, London; 27(bottom) Novosti. Collections: 9(bottom)
Brian Shuel. Corbis-Bettmann: 18, 19(bottom), 20, 21(bottom). E.T. Archive: 35(top). Mary Evans Picture Library:
11(bottom), 19(top), 21(top), 25, 32(bottom). Hulton Getty Picture Collection: 6, 7(top), 8, 9(top), 22, 24(bottom),
26, 27(top), 28(bottom), 29, 31(top), 34, 36(top), 37, 39(top), 39(bottom), 40(bottom), 42, 44, 45(top). Kobal
Collection: 4 London Films. North Wind Picture Archives: 15(top), 15(bottom), 16, 17(top), 17(bottom).
Popperfoto: 5(top), 10, 13(top), 35(bottom), 38, 41. Z. Radovan, Jerusalem: 45(bottom). Rex Features: 5(bottom),
28(top) Sipa/Tom Haley; 40(top).

Words in **bold** appear in the glossary on page 46.

CONTENTS

INTRODUCTION

Throughout history, rulers, governments, and armies have sent undercover agents to spy on their enemies. Some spies were motivated by greed, but others believed they were fighting evil.

The first spies

One of the earliest undercover agents was Guy Fawkes. He attempted to blow up the English king James I and his Parliament in 1605. In the late seventeenth and early eighteenth centuries, Daniel Defoe, more famous as the author of *Robinson Crusoe*, spied for Queen Anne and King George I.

Undercover in America

In America, too, undercover agents made their mark. During the American Revolution, soldier Benedict Arnold sold his country's military secrets to Great Britain. In the nineteenth century, Harriet Tubman helped slaves escape to the North.

War spies

The two major wars of the twentieth century provided numerous opportunities for undercover work. The glamorous Mata Hari was a spy during World War I (1914–1918), while many agents opposed the **Nazis** in World War II (1939–1945).

An atmospheric scene from *The Third Man*, a film about spies in Austria set after World War II.

The French Resistance worked undercover to locate German troops.

Anti-Nazi plots

In Germany, Claus von Stauffenberg plotted to assassinate Nazi leader Adolf Hitler. In Hungary, Raoul Wallenberg helped the Jewish victims of the Nazis escape. In Yugoslavia, Tito organized **guerrilla** bands to ambush the Germans, while in France, Odette Churchill worked with the **resistance** against the enemy.

U-2 and ER-2 spy planes of the United States Air Force fly over San Francisco's Golden Gate Bridge.

The Cold War

After World War II, spying increased as **Communist** and non-Communist countries tried to find out one another's secrets. This political struggle is known as the **Cold War**. One famous spy of the period was Kim Philby, who gave British secrets away to the Soviet Union.

Modern spies

Today sophisticated satellites and spy planes can reveal some secrets, for example, about troop movements, from above the ground. As a result, the role of the spy has changed. But there will always be a place for the person who, with cunning and skill, can discover information that governments and individuals would much rather hide.

GUY FAWKES

1570–1606

Guy Fawkes, the Catholic conspirator who almost blew up Parliament in 1605.

Guy Fawkes was one of the first undercover agents whose deeds were recorded. In early seventeenth-century England, which was ruled by the **Protestant** king James I, Fawkes risked his life to fight for the rights of **Roman Catholics**.

In 1534, following Pope Clement VII's refusal to grant him a divorce, the English king, Henry VIII, broke away from the Roman Catholic Church. He then made himself head of the Church of England. Henry remained a Catholic for the most part, but he never again recognized the Pope's authority. He persecuted Catholics who would not accept him as Supreme Head of the Church of England.

Protestant and Catholic

Following Henry's death in 1547, the situation changed. The ideas of the **Reformation** grew popular, and many people became Protestants. During the reign of the Protestant queen Elizabeth I (1558–1603), anti-Catholic feeling spread. After her death, the Protestant James I became king. Since he was the son of the Catholic Mary Queen of Scots, many Catholics hoped for better treatment. But James allowed their persecution to continue.

The men who designed the Gunpowder Plot to kill
James I. Fawkes is third from the right.

Guy Fawkes

Guy Fawkes was born in York in 1570.
He was brought up as a Protestant until
his father died in 1579. Then his mother
married a Catholic, and Fawkes adopted
his stepfather's religion. During the
sixteenth century, Catholic Spain ruled the
Netherlands, whose Protestant people were
fighting for independence. In 1593 Fawkes
left England to join the Spanish Army.

Return to England

In 1604, a year after James I became king,
Fawkes was asked to come back to England
by fellow Catholic Thomas Winter. On his
return, he saw how poorly Catholics were
treated and decided to do something about
the situation. An opportunity soon arose.
During a meeting at the house of another
Catholic, Robert Catesby, Fawkes was
invited to join a plot to assassinate James I.

The Reformation

In 1517 a monk named Martin Luther posted a
list of complaints on a church door in Wittenberg,
Germany. He was angry about the wealth and
power of the Roman Catholic Church. Many people
supported him, and they became known as
Protestants. Some Protestants destroyed statues in
Catholic churches (below) because they believed
the statues were **idols**. The movement that Luther
began is known as the Reformation because he
wanted to reform the Roman Catholic Church.

The Gunpowder Plot

The group decided that the only way to stop anti-Catholic persecution was to blow up the king and his parliament with gunpowder. They agreed to do this on November 5, 1605, when James I was to open the new parliamentary session. This Catholic conspiracy later became known as the Gunpowder Plot.

Change of plans

The plotters rented a house near the Parliament buildings, then tried to dig a tunnel through to their cellars. But this was more difficult than expected because the walls of the house were extremely thick. So instead, Catesby found a cellar to rent directly underneath Parliament, and the group hid the gunpowder there.

Cellar keeper

Guy Fawkes agreed to look after the cellar and to light the fuse that would set off the explosion. He hid the gunpowder under firewood and coal. Then, adopting the name of John Johnson, he pretended that his job was to look after the piles of fuel.

Seated on his throne and dressed in his royal robes, King James I directs a meeting of Parliament.

Bonfire Night

On the night of November 5, 1605, people loyal to James I celebrated the failure of the Gunpowder Plot by lighting bonfires. Some made straw figures of Guy Fawkes and burned them on top of the fires. To this day, British people still burn a "guy" and set off fireworks on November 5. Children sing:

Remember, remember,
The fifth of November,
Gunpowder, treason, and plot.
I see no reason
Why gunpowder treason
Should ever be forgot.

Anonymous note

One plotter, Francis Tresham, discovered that members of his family would be at the opening of Parliament on November 5. He begged the other conspirators to postpone their plan, but they refused. Instead, they promised to warn Tresham's family two days in advance. But Tresham sent an anonymous note to his cousin, Lord Monteagle, telling him to stay away. Monteagle showed the king, who ordered a search of Parliament on November 4.

Discovery and arrest

The **Yeomen of the Guard** searched the cellars twice. On the first occasion, they discovered only Guy Fawkes looking after his piles of firewood and coal. But when they returned at eleven o'clock that night, they found the gunpowder hidden underneath the fuel. Guy Fawkes was immediately placed under arrest.

Guy Fawkes placing a trail of gunpowder underneath Parliament just hours before his capture.

Trial and execution

Guy Fawkes was tortured on the **rack**. Some say he bravely refused to give away the names of the other plotters. Others claim he named them. He signed a confession, and in January 1606 was tried, then **hanged, drawn, and quartered**. Seven men were hanged along with Fawkes.

A place in history

Guy Fawkes was a courageous man, who was prepared to die for his religious beliefs. He has become one of the most famous undercover agents in English history for his involvement in the Gunpowder Plot.

DANIEL DEFOE

1660–1731

Daniel Defoe is among the greatest names in English literature. Today he is best known as the author of *Robinson Crusoe*, but he was also one of the British monarchy's finest secret agents.

Defoe was born in London in 1660. His original last name was simply Foe, but he changed it to the more fashionable Defoe in about 1703. Defoe's father was a wealthy, hardworking butcher and **chandler**, who had his son trained to be a Presbyterian minister. But Defoe decided against this career, and by 1683 had set himself up in business as a **hosiery** merchant.

A second career

In the 1680s, Defoe started a second career as a writer on politics and religion. He was passionately opposed to the Roman Catholic king, James II, and in 1685, he took part in the Duke of Monmouth's rebellion against him. But Defoe was an enthusiastic supporter of the Protestant William III, who replaced James in 1689. During these years, Defoe ran various unsuccessful businesses, but he also spent much of his time writing pamphlets in favor of William.

Daniel Defoe led two separate lives. He was both a brilliant writer and a successful undercover agent for Queen Anne and later King George I.

Secret agent

While Defoe was in prison, his tile-making business collapsed, and he was left with large debts. He appealed for help, and Robert Harley, Earl of Oxford, came to his rescue. Harley arranged his release on the understanding that Defoe would work for him as a pamphlet writer and secret agent. The earl thought Defoe would be highly suitable for the work because he was a trained and careful observer, who knew how to record all he saw and heard.

People normally threw rotten fruit at criminals in the pillory. But they showered Defoe with flowers.

In the pillory

In 1703 Defoe caused himself serious trouble when he wrote a pamphlet that criticized the government. He was found guilty of **libel**, fined, imprisoned, and forced to stand in the **pillory** three times. Defoe managed to turn his punishment into a triumph by writing a poem called *Hymn to the Pillory*. Many people bought copies. They also showed their support by covering Defoe's pillory with flowers and drinking to his health.

The Glorious Revolution

When the Catholic James II fled Great Britain in 1688, Parliament offered the throne to his daughter, Mary, and her husband, William of Orange, a prince of the Netherlands. Both were Protestants. William and Mary invaded and became joint rulers. But William said he had no **divine right** to be king, and would only accept the position if Parliament offered it to him. It did so in 1689 (below), and the monarchy became constitutional, or subject to the law. This change in the relationship between Crown and Parliament is known as the Glorious Revolution.

A new monarch

In 1702 William III died. Anne, Protestant daughter of the Catholic James II, then became queen. Anne's father had died a year earlier. But his Catholic son, James Stuart, was still alive in France. Many people, particularly in Scotland, believed he was the true heir to the throne.

The Jacobite threat

The supporters of James Stuart were known as Jacobites, and they caused Queen Anne serious concern. So she decided to use Defoe, who supported her, to collect evidence against them. He later wrote that the queen had employed him "in several honorable, though secret, services."

No hiding place

Defoe's role was to travel all over Great Britain, writing reports on public opinion. He was particularly successful in discovering Jacobite hiding places. He even managed to spend time in their homes, where he listened to their conversations.

Ambitious plan

The success of his undercover operations made Defoe a greatly respected figure in Queen Anne's court. So he wrote to Robert Harley with an ambitious plan to establish a new secret service, with more agents. Defoe believed this would allow the Queen's ministers to receive useful information from all parts of the country.

Robinson Crusoe

At the age of sixty, after producing many pamphlets on political and religious subjects, Daniel Defoe wrote *The Life and Strange Surprising Adventures of Robinson Crusoe of York, Mariner*, now known simply as *Robinson Crusoe*. This exciting tale of shipwreck and adventure on a tropical island was inspired by the true adventures of Alexander Selkirk, a Scottish sailor. It is regarded as the first English novel, and since its publication in 1719, it has become one of the most famous and popular books of all time.

Success and failure

The tour was the high point of Defoe's career as a secret agent. The last years of his life were spent fighting legal battles over old debts. Historians believe that Daniel Defoe, the author of some of the most famous books in the English language, and perhaps the founder of the modern secret service, died hiding from his **creditors**.

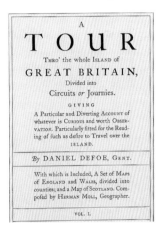

The title page of Defoe's travel book (left). The book included maps of England, Wales, and (below) Scotland. Perhaps Defoe used them to find secret Jacobite hideouts.

James Stuart, the son of the Catholic king James II. Jacobites believed he, not his sister Anne, should have become the monarch when William III died.

Tour of Great Britain

Following Queen Anne's death in 1714, George I came to the throne. During his reign, Defoe was even more successful. As the Jacobite threat continued to grow, he was sent on a tour of the kingdom to collect information. Defoe was now the king's main secret agent. He traveled under various aliases, or false names, and organized a network of agents.

Traveling writer

During his travels, Defoe posed as a writer, and he was able to uncover various groups of Jacobite rebels. But he also wrote a successful book, *A Tour Thro' the Whole Island of Great Britain*, published in 1726.

BENEDICT ARNOLD

1741–1801

During the American Revolution, many famous people, including George Washington, fought to liberate their country from British rule. But a few Americans helped the British. Perhaps the most infamous of these traitors was Benedict Arnold.

Arnold was born in Norwich, Connecticut, in 1741. As a young man, he ran away to fight for the British in the **French and Indian War**. Then in 1762, after his parents died, Arnold moved to New Haven. There he set himself up as a **druggist**, bookseller, and trader. He soon became a very wealthy man.

The American Revolution

Arnold also became captain of a **militia** company. When the American Revolution started in 1775, he led his men to Fort Ticonderoga in New York, a British base. With the help of Ethan Allen, another militia leader, he captured the fort and was made a colonel. Arnold then went to George Washington, the American commander, with a plan to invade Canada and capture the British post of Quebec. Washington agreed, and Arnold and 1,100 men set out on the long march north.

Benedict Arnold sold American secrets to the British during the American Revolution.

Failure and disappointment

After two months marching, Arnold's exhausted soldiers arrived in Quebec. They launched an attack in December 1775, but were unable to capture the post. Arnold was wounded in the leg but maintained a **blockade** around the city. He was made a brigadier general for his heroic efforts.

George Washington knew that Arnold was a superb commander and used him in several campaigns. But other commanders were jealous of Arnold's success, and they promoted a junior officer over his head. Arnold was furious at this treatment.

Another battle

In 1777 Arnold was again in the thick of battle at Saratoga, near New York, and managed to repel the British attack. But his horse was killed during the fighting, and he suffered a wound in the same leg that had been shot in Quebec.

The assault on Quebec

Benedict Arnold's invasion of Canada took place in the bitter cold of winter. He marched his troops up through the state of Maine, then crossed the border and advanced on Quebec in a blinding snowstorm. There he met up with another American force under the leadership of the Irish-born general Richard Montgomery. But even their combined efforts were not enough to defeat the British forces. Arnold, though injured, lived to fight again. Montgomery was killed during the attack on December 31, 1775.

Fierce fighting between the Americans (in blue) and the British (in red) at Concord Bridge in 1775.

Life in Philadelphia

Disabled from his wounds, Arnold was placed in command of the city of Philadelphia in 1778. He then started to live extravagantly and run up huge debts. This led him into corrupt business deals to raise money. At the same time, Arnold was becoming more friendly with families who supported the British. His first wife, Margaret Mansfield, with whom he had three sons, had died in 1775. In 1779 he married Margaret Shippen, the 18-year-old daughter of a pro-British American.

The road to treason

The combination of family and financial pressures led Arnold to contact the British authorities. He hoped that they would pay for information about the American forces. Arnold told them about a planned American invasion of Canada, and gave away several other important military secrets.

Major John André

Major John André was Benedict Arnold's British contact. On the night of September 21, 1780, Arnold met him to pass on the secrets of West Point's defenses (right). But the following day, the Americans arrested André and charged him with spying. On October 2, 1780, the British soldier was hanged. A monument was erected to his memory in Westminster Abbey, London, where his remains are buried. He is the only spy ever to have been honored in this way.

West Point

Arnold also offered to surrender the military post of West Point in New York, of which he was commander. He asked for £20,000 and a job in the British Army in return.

The city of Philadelphia, where Arnold became military commander in 1778.

Exile in London

Arnold lived in London for twenty years. King George III welcomed him, but did not offer him an official post. Instead, Arnold earned his living by importing West Indian goods. Both he and his family were excluded from London social life because of his spy activities. Arnold died a bitter man in 1801.

Notorious traitor

Benedict Arnold might easily have been remembered as one of the greatest commanders of the American Revolution. But because of his resentment toward the army he served and his extravagant living and personal greed, he is one of his country's most notorious traitors.

Discovery and flight

In 1780 Arnold's plan was detected by the Americans, and he fled to the British side. He received only £6,315 as financial reward for his treachery, but was made a brigadier general in the British Army. Once in his new post, he led raids on the homes of many former friends. Arnold tried to persuade other Americans to join him, but only 28 were willing to desert. Following the British surrender in 1781, Arnold sailed to England with his wife and children.

Arnold escaped on horseback after his plot to surrender West Point was discovered.

HARRIET TUBMAN

1820–1913

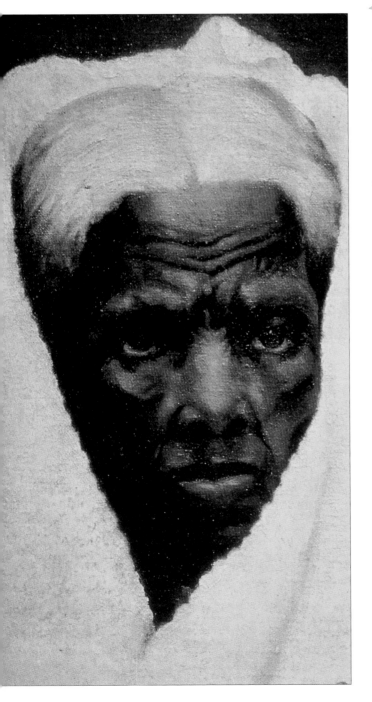

Harriet Tubman was born in 1820 on a plantation in the southern United States. She was named Araminta but was known as Harriet, her mother's name. Like her parents, brothers, and sisters, Harriet was a slave.

The plantation was a world in itself. The slaveowner lived in "the big house," as the slaves called it, while the slaves lived in "slave row," a line of small cabins that were more suitable for animals than humans. Surrounding these were the cotton fields where the slaves worked. On the cotton plantations, slaves labored in terrible conditions. They had no rights, and a slaveowner could separate a mother from her child or a husband from his wife at any time, simply by selling one of them.

Early life

Harriet started working as a maid at the age of five. She looked after her owner's children until she was 12, when she was sent to work in the fields. A year later, Harriet tried to prevent a foreman from punishing one of the other slaves. He beat her so hard for interfering that he fractured her skull. Although she recovered, Harriet suffered from black-outs, or sudden losses of consciousness, for the rest of her life.

Harriet Tubman escaped from slavery herself, then led hundreds of other slaves to freedom.

The comfortable and spacious "big house" of a wealthy Mississippi plantation owner.

Useful knowledge

Like most American slaves, Harriet never learned to read or write. But her father, Benjamin Ross, taught her how to find food and survive in the woods beyond the plantations. This knowledge was very useful to her in later years.

Marriage and escape

In 1844 Harriet's owner let her marry John Tubman, a freed slave. Throughout their marriage, Harriet was afraid of being sold to a new owner in the Deep South. But her husband did not share her concern. In 1849 Harriet was about to be sold, but she escaped to Philadelphia in the North. She returned a few months later to find that her husband had remarried.

The Cotton Kingdom

Before the nineteenth century, cotton-growing in the United States was limited to a few coastal states in the Deep South. This was because the only type of cotton that could be processed easily would not grow elsewhere. But in 1793, Eli Whitney invented the **cotton gin**, which made it possible to process plants that could grow inland. Gins were installed in many barns such as this (right), and cotton-growing spread rapidly westward. The cotton-growing region became known as the Cotton Kingdom.

The Underground Railroad

In 1850 Harriet returned to the South again to help her sister and two children escape to the North. A year later, she fetched her brother's family. All of them fled on the Underground Railroad, a network of road and sea escape routes between the South and the North. The Railroad was operated by ex-slaves, known as "conductors." The slaves were "passengers," and the homes they hid in were "stations." Harriet became a conductor and helped 300 slaves reach the North and Canada, where slavery was illegal. A $40,000 reward was offered for her capture.

Fighting slavery

In the early 1850s, Harriet lived in Canada, where she acted as adviser to antislavery campaigner John Brown. In 1858 she moved to New York, but still worked hard for antislavery groups. In the 1860 elections, the antislavery candidate Abraham Lincoln became president.

The Civil War

The South wanted to keep slaves, so opposed Lincoln. Finally, some of the southern states withdrew from the United States. This led to the Civil War (1861–1865), which the North won. Harriet was active in the northern army as a nurse and spy. She commanded a group of soldiers that freed over 750 slaves. This was the only military campaign in American history to be led by a woman.

Harriet Tubman (far left) with some of the slaves she helped to escape.

House slaves waiting to be sold. They would soon be the "property" of rich owners in New Orleans.

After the war

In 1869 Harriet married Nathan Davies. The couple worked together for many years. They founded schools for freed slaves, where they taught and preached, raised funds for black people, and set up a home for the poor and elderly.

Women's rights

Harriet also promoted the rights of black women and helped to found the National Association of Colored Women in 1896. At its first convention, she was enthusiastically congratulated for her bravery on the Underground Railroad and during the Civil War, as well as for her stand on women's rights. After a lifetime of hard work and struggle, Harriet died in 1913.

The Moses of her people

Harriet Tubman was known by many names. The most famous was "the Moses of her people" because, like Moses in the Old Testament of the Bible, she led slaves to freedom. Her ideals were summed up in this statement: "There was one of two things that I had a right to, liberty or death; if I could not have one, I would have the other; for no man should take me alive..."

Reconstruction

After the Civil War ended, the southern states had to be reunited with the United States. At the same time, former slaves and former slaveowners had to face a new way of life. The period in which all these changes took place is called Reconstruction (1865–1877). At first, the government helped African Americans find work, build homes, and study (right). The U.S. **Constitution** was also changed to grant them equal rights. But gradually, white people began to take back their power.

MATA HARI

1876–1917

The most glamorous spy ever was Margarete Gertrud Zelle. She is remembered now as Mata Hari. Margarete was born in 1876 in the Netherlands, the daughter of a merchant. She grew up to be a beautiful and adventurous young woman, with a great zest for life.

Margarete showed her sense of adventure at the age of 17, when she answered a **lonely-hearts** advertisement. This was how she met her future husband, John MacLeod, a 38-year-old officer from the Dutch East Indies. The couple married and went to live in Java, an island in the Indian Ocean. Margarete was fascinated by the local customs, especially dancing.

An unhappy marriage

Margarete soon realized that her decision to marry had been a mistake. Her husband drank too much. He also beat her and their children, a son who died while still very young, and a daughter. In 1901 the whole family returned to the Netherlands. A year later, MacLeod deserted his wife and took their daughter with him. Margarete went to court and won **custody**. But her husband refused to support them, and soon mother and daughter were penniless. So Margarete had to leave her child with relatives.

Mata Hari in the costume of a Hindu princess.

Javanese dancing

As a young woman in Java, Mata Hari watched the local female dancers. She was always intrigued by their elaborate and colorful costumes, especially the headdresses, which often included feathers and flowers. The women danced slowly, using their hands and eyes to emphasize different emotions. Mata Hari used these dancing styles when she worked in Paris in 1904.

The Folies Bergère was the most famous nightclub in Paris during Mata Hari's time.

A new life in Paris

By 1904 Margarete still had no money. But she remained adventurous, so decided to go to Paris in France. There she became an exotic dancer, using her knowledge of the dances she had seen in Java. It was at this time that she took the name *Mata Hari*, Malay words meaning "eye of the day."

Mata Hari was an enormous success and danced in France, Spain, and Germany. She was praised as one of the most beautiful women in Europe, and many important men sought her company.

World War I

When World War I started in 1914, Mata Hari was living in Berlin. She had moved there to be with her companion, the German chief of police. He persuaded her to spy on the important men she knew. Useful information was passed on to the German secret service. At the same time, Mata Hari was having a relationship with a captain connected to the French secret service and was supplying confidential information to France. But the Germans also knew she was a double agent.

Test of loyalty

As a result of her double-crossing, no one trusted Mata Hari. Wherever she went in Europe, there was always a member of one or more secret services following her. She returned to France, but the French decided to **deport** her. Pleading with them for mercy, Mata Hari again offered her services as a secret agent. To test her loyalty, the French sent her on a mission to Brussels, the capital of Belgium. There she was employed to spy on the occupying German forces.

A scene from the 1932 film *Mata Hari*, with Greta Garbo as the glamorous international spy.

Code-breaking

Coded messages, often sent by **telegraph** operators like these in France (right), were used in World War I. But the codes were frequently broken. The breaking of the code used in the 1917 Zimmermann telegram had dramatic consequences. The telegram was sent by the Germans to the Mexicans, asking them to enter the war by fighting the United States. British agents intercepted and decoded the telegram, then sent it to U.S. president Woodrow Wilson. He told the American people what the telegram contained, and their outrage was one of the reasons the United States entered the war.

Caught in a trap

Despite her best efforts, Mata Hari could not get any information from her German contacts because of her reputation. So she traveled on to the Netherlands and then by ship to Spain. When she arrived, German agents decided to betray her to the French. They deliberately sent a message to Spain using a code they knew the French had broken. In the message, the Germans ordered Mata Hari to return to France. She did so, making it clear to the French that she was still obeying German orders.

Trial and sentence

Mata Hari was arrested in Paris on February 13, 1917, and charged with spying. Her trial lasted two days, and at the end she was sentenced to death. Many people appealed to the French government for mercy. But on October 15, 1917, Mata Hari was shot by a firing squad in Vincennes.

Why did she die?

Historians believe that Mata Hari did not give the Germans information of any value. The French government knew this, so may have executed her only because she was an embarrassment. They may also have used her trial to distract attention from France's lack of success in the war at that time.

Strange truth

The glamorous, headstrong Dutchwoman Mata Hari is one of the most memorable undercover agents in history. This is strange since none of the secret information she passed on proved to be significant.

This painting of Mata Hari's execution appeared on a book cover in 1917, the year of her death.

TITO

1892–1980

Most undercover agents spend their whole lives working in secret. Yet the Communist and wartime resistance leader Tito eventually became the president of his country, the former Yugoslavia.

Tito's original name was Josip Broz. He was born in 1892 in Kumrovec, in northwestern Croatia, which at that time was part of the **Austro-Hungarian Empire**. Broz came from a poor peasant family and was the seventh of 15 children. At the age of 15, he was apprenticed to a locksmith in the town of Sisak. Later, as a young man, he was employed as a metalworker in Austria, Bohemia, and Germany.

World War I

Traveling across Europe as a teenager, Broz saw how harshly working people were treated. He joined the Social Democratic Party of Croatia to fight against these injustices. But his plans to improve working conditions were pushed aside by war.

World War I broke out in 1914, and Broz was **drafted** into the Austro-Hungarian Army. He fought bravely and was given a medal for his courage. But in 1915, he was stabbed by a **Cossack**'s lance and captured by the Russian Army.

Tito, the wartime resistance fighter who became premier and later president of Yugoslavia.

In 1915, during World War I, Tito was wounded by Cossack troops like these.

The Russian Revolution

During the Russian Revolution of 1917, Broz was released from prison. Inspired by this great Communist uprising, he, too, became a Communist. When he returned home to Croatia in 1920, he helped establish the Communist Party of Yugoslavia.

Communism in Yugoslavia

Broz started to work undercover to get his new party into power. Because the Communist Party was an illegal organization in Yugoslavia, many other people worked for it outside the country. But Broz was quite different. He deliberately worked within Yugoslavia's borders. Gradually, he managed to gain support and organize the party on a national basis.

New name

Broz also traveled to Moscow, Paris, Prague, and Vienna to establish contacts with foreign Communists. At home and abroad he used aliases to disguise his identity. In 1928 he was imprisoned for his work. A year later he was released, and he adopted one alias, Tito, as his own name.

Communism

Communism is a political theory that was devised by German philosophers Karl Marx and Friedrich Engels. It states that property should be owned by the state rather than individuals, to bring about equality for all. Following a revolution in 1917 (below), the first country to adopt Communism was Russia (later called the Soviet Union). Some other countries freely adopted Communism, while more were forced to by the Soviets. In 1991 the Soviet Union broke up, and many former Communist lands introduced democracy.

World War II

Tito's talents as an undercover agent were used even more successfully during World War II (1939–1945). On April 6, 1941, Germany invaded Yugoslavia. So Tito issued a proclamation calling all Yugoslavians to repel the Nazi invaders. Then he organized guerrilla bands to lead the fight. At first, these consisted of just a few men and women – the Partisans. Tito himself led them into battle against the Germans and their Italian allies.

Ambush attacks

Tito soon gained military success by repeatedly ambushing the Nazis, then quickly retreating to the hills and woods. The Partisans won so many battles that the Nazi leader, Adolf Hitler, sent thousands of extra German troops to Yugoslavia to hunt them down and kill them.

In this 1944 scene, wounded Partisans are transported by cart to hideouts in the hills.

The breakup of Yugoslavia

At the end of World War I, in 1918, three **Slav** peoples living in southeast Europe, the Serbs, Croats, and Slovenes, created a new country called Yugoslavia. They were ruled over by a Serbian king.

When World War II ended, in 1945, Yugoslavia became a **federation** of six republics, with Tito as ruler. When he died in 1980, the different Slav peoples each began to demand independence. In the early 1990s, fighting broke out, and three of the republics — Croatia, Slovenia, and Bosnia-Herzegovina — finally broke away to form independent states.

Today much of the region lies in ruins. These inhabitants of Sarajevo (left) stand amid the rubble to recall the happier times of 1984, when their city hosted the Winter Olympics.

Long struggle

Tito's guerrilla groups defeated the German Army. By 1944 he also had the support of the **Allies**. But thousands of Partisans died in the struggle. Tito himself was wounded and almost taken prisoner.

From guerrilla to president

Tito became **premier** of Yugoslavia in 1945. Eight years later, he was elected president. Tito led Yugoslavia successfully for over thirty years, until he died on May 4, 1980, after a long illness. The young peasant from Croatia had become one of the most famous leaders in the world. Millions mourned his death and remembered his brave fight to keep Yugoslavia free and independent.

President Tito with President John F. Kennedy during a visit to the United States in 1963.

CLAUS VON STAUFFENBERG

1907–1944

As a member of an old and distinguished German family, Count Claus von Stauffenberg made a very unlikely conspirator. But he is famous as the man who almost killed Germany's notorious war leader Adolf Hitler.

Stauffenberg was born in November 1907 near Stuttgart, in Germany. His family had worked in the royal courts for hundreds of years, and he could trace his ancestry back to the fourteenth century. As a boy, he went to the Ludwig Eberhard Gymnasium (grammar school) in Stuttgart. There he was taught that as a nobleman he had a duty both to lead and to serve his country.

Army training

After leaving school, Stauffenberg joined a top **Bavarian** cavalry regiment. He quickly established himself as a promising soldier, and was soon promoted to the rank of First Lieutenant. In 1936 Stauffenberg was sent to the famous Berlin War Academy. His outstanding performance there meant that he would eventually be appointed to the General Staff, the group of senior generals who ran the German Army.

Claus von Stauffenberg, a young officer who decided that Hitler had to die if Germany was to avoid defeat in World War II.

The causes of World War II

When World War I ended in 1918, the victors (Great Britain, France, Russia, and the United States) took over all Germany's prewar territories. In the 1930s, the Nazis set out to recover them. Between 1936 and 1939, Germany invaded the Rhineland, Austria, and Czechoslovakia. The British and French policy of **appeasement** allowed this. Then German troops assembled in Berlin (left) and invaded Poland. Great Britain and France had warned this would mean war, and it was declared in September 1939.

World War II

In the 1930s, Stauffenberg became very concerned that Germany was planning to go to war with the rest of Europe. In 1939 his worries were confirmed when Great Britain and France declared war on Germany because it had invaded Poland. This was the beginning of World War II (1939–1945), which eventually involved most of the countries in the world. For the first three years of the war, Stauffenberg served in the Soviet Union, which was then Germany's ally. But in 1941, Germany declared war on the Soviet Union.

Ready to act

Stauffenberg believed that Germany could not win the war without Soviet help, so he became convinced that Hitler was leading his country to defeat. He was also greatly concerned by the brutality of Hitler's methods. In 1942 Stauffenberg decided that Hitler had to die. In the fall of that year, he announced: "It isn't a question of telling the **Führer** the truth but killing him, and I'm ready to do the dirty work."

The harsh winter of 1942 forced the Nazis to leave the Soviet Union.

Wounded in Africa

In January 1943, before he was able to make any plans, Stauffenberg was assigned to North Africa. Three months later, he was wounded in an attack by an enemy plane. He lost his right hand, two fingers of his left hand, and his right eye, and suffered injuries to his knee and ear. He was sent to Germany for medical treatment.

The plot begins

Most officers who visited Stauffenberg in the hospital agreed that Hitler should be assassinated. Without him, they believed, Germany could start peace negotiations with Great Britain, the Soviet Union, and the United States, which had entered the war in 1941. But the plotters needed someone to get close enough to Hitler to kill him. This problem was solved in May 1944, when Stauffenberg became a **chief of staff**. His new post meant that he would have frequent access to Germany's leader.

Hitler greets one of his generals as Stauffenberg (far left) looks on.

Adolf Hitler

Adolf Hitler, shown here saluting the Nazi Army (left), was born in 1889. He fought in World War I (1914–1918), which Germany lost. In 1923 he wrote a book called *Mein Kampf (My Struggle),* which blamed the Jews for Germany's problems and stated that the country needed a strong leader. In 1933 he took on that role.

Hitler's ambition to conquer Europe led to World War II (1939–1945), in which Germany was again defeated. Millions of people died as a result of the war, including six million Jews and others in **concentration camps**. Hitler escaped trial as a war criminal by committing suicide in his underground bunker in May 1945.

The assassination attempt

The conspirators' plan was to place a bomb in a briefcase and leave it under the table at Hitler's headquarters in Rastenburg. Then Stauffenberg was to fly to Berlin and set up a government. On July 20, 1944, Stauffenberg planted the bomb. It went off, killing four people, but Hitler suffered only bruises and burns. This was largely due to a wooden table leg that had obstructed the explosion.

Confusion and failure

Stauffenberg managed to reach an airfield and took off half an hour after the bomb exploded. But his fellow plotters in Berlin failed to act quickly. There was so much confusion about whether the German leader was alive or dead that the long-planned overthrow ended early.

Arrest and death

That night, a group of officers who had remained loyal to Hitler arrested Stauffenberg and the other conspirators. A **court-martial** was quickly held, and all the plotters were condemned to death. They were taken down to a courtyard and shot by a firing squad. As Stauffenberg fell to the ground, he shouted: "Long live sacred Germany!"

World War II continued for another year, until Germany surrendered in May 1945. We can only guess how many lives might have been saved if Stauffenberg's plot had succeeded.

Nazi officers visit Hitler's headquarters after Stauffenberg's assassination attempt.

KIM PHILBY

1912–1988

Why do some undercover agents betray their own country? Often it is with the belief that their treachery will help their nation rather than harm it.

The most notorious group of agents to betray Great Britain were the Cambridge spies – Guy Burgess, Donald Maclean, Kim Philby, Anthony Blunt, and John Cairncross. They were all at Cambridge University during the 1930s, and believed that only the Soviet Union could stop the threat of the Nazis in Germany.

Early life

The most famous member of this group was Harold Adrian Russell Philby. He was nicknamed "Kim," after an Indian boy-spy in the novel of the same name by Rudyard Kipling. Philby was born in India in 1912. His father, Harry St. John Philby, worked for the Indian Civil Service, although he later became a famous explorer. As a young man, Kim had a privileged education at Westminster School, London, and Trinity College, Cambridge. Philby met Guy Burgess and Donald Maclean while at Cambridge, and learned that they, too, were strong supporters of Soviet Communism.

Kim Philby became the most notorious and successful of the spies who met at Cambridge University during the 1930s.

Philby developed his Communist ideas in student rooms like these in the 1930s, in Cambridge.

KGB recruits

The pro-Communist ideas of this group were noticed by the KGB, the Soviet secret service, which recruited them as spies. The KGB believed that these men would soon hold jobs in which they would have access to information useful to the Soviet Union.

Wartime work

For Kim Philby, this proved to be true. The Soviets recruited him in 1933, and in 1939 he was appointed senior correspondent for *The Times* newspaper. In the same year, at the start of World War II, he was sent to France with the **British Expeditionary Force**. Then in 1940, British **intelligence** asked Philby to work for them. They wanted him to take responsibility for sabotage, **subversion**, and propaganda. Philby had fooled them into believing that he was a patriotic Englishman, when all the time he was working as a Soviet spy.

The Cold War

When World War II ended in 1945, a different kind of war started. This was the Cold War, a political conflict between the Soviet Union and its Communist allies in Eastern Europe, and the United States and its non-Communist allies in Western Europe. The conflict was symbolized by the Berlin Wall (right), which was built in 1961 and divided Communist East Berlin from non-Communist West Berlin. The wall was dismantled in 1989, and after the collapse of the Soviet Union in 1991, the Cold War ended, and relations between the sides improved.

Double agent

During World War II, Philby worked as a spy for the British and the Soviets. The British even wanted him to parachute into occupied Europe to spy for them. But Philby had a speech disorder. This was unsuitable for a spy on enemy territory, because it would make him stand out.

After the war

In 1946, a year after the war ended, Philby was put in charge of British and American spying operations in the Soviet Union. The KGB were delighted because he was able to supply them with precious information and at the same time destroy information that might damage Soviet interests.

Like Philby, Guy Burgess (below, left) and Donald Maclean were recruited by the KGB. Together they formed a highly successful spy network.

MI6

In 1940 Kim Philby joined MI6, which stands for Military Intelligence, Section 6. Today this British government agency is known as the Secret Intelligence Service. Its role is to work abroad gathering information about other countries, but it is based in this large building in London (above). MI6's sister department, MI5, operates within the United Kingdom carrying out counterintelligence. This is designed to prevent foreign governments from spying. MI5 is also involved in antiterrorism work.

Washington mission

Philby was trusted so much that he was sent to Washington, D.C., three years later. His mission was to help the CIA, the American secret service, to spy on the Soviets, and to establish relations between British and United States intelligence. He was now one of the most important spies in the world. But an incident involving Burgess and Maclean soon changed the situation completely.

Growing suspicions

Philby knew that the Americans suspected Maclean of spying, and in 1951 he sent Burgess to London to tell him. Burgess warned Maclean, then both men escaped to the Soviet Union. This threw suspicion on Philby, because Burgess had been with him in Washington. For the next ten years, many people suspected Philby of spying for the Soviets. Although nothing could be proved against him, the suspicions alone meant that he had to leave his post in Washington and return to London. But he was soon spying for the British again.

Final discovery

Eventually, Philby's luck ran out. In 1961 George Blake, another British spy working for the Soviets, was arrested. During his interrogation he named Philby as an agent. The authorities were so embarrassed by this discovery that Philby was not arrested.

Flight to the Soviet Union

The British hoped that Philby would escape, to avoid the need for a trial that would publicly confirm people's suspicions. They were not to be disappointed. Philby fled to Moscow in 1961 and lived there until his death in May 1988. He continued to work for the KGB, and he was buried in Moscow with full **military honors**.

Betrayer, or betrayed?

Like the other Cambridge spies, Kim Philby never saw himself as a traitor to his country. He believed that Great Britain had betrayed him simply by not becoming a Communist country, like the Soviet Union.

Kim Philby striding through Moscow in 1968. He lived in the Soviet capital for 27 years, until his death in 1988.

ODETTE CHURCHILL

1912–1995

Some of the bravest people to serve during World War II were undercover agents. These men and women volunteered for dangerous duties in occupied Europe. Among them was Odette Churchill.

Odette Churchill's original name was Odette Brailly. She was born in France in 1912, and she was educated at a convent school in Amiens. In 1931 Brailly married Roy Sanson, an English friend of her father's. The couple then moved to London, where they had three daughters.

Going undercover

World War II began in 1939, and Odette's husband went away to serve in the armed forces. In 1942 Odette decided to move out of London with her daughters. Once settled in Somerset, she answered a government appeal for French speakers.

Nothing in Odette's background made it likely that she would become a secret agent. When she responded to the appeal, Odette thought she would be working as a translator. But the authorities recognized her courage and patriotism, and recruited her to carry out undercover work.

Frenchwoman Odette Churchill became one of the most courageous spies of World War II.

German troops arriving in the town of Arras, in northern France, in May 1940.

The Gestapo

The Gestapo was the Nazi secret police force. It was originally made up of a small number of Hitler's personal bodyguards. But when he became Führer, the Gestapo grew bigger and more powerful. After 1936, it was led on Hitler's behalf by another high-ranking Nazi, Heinrich Himmler. These two Gestapo members (below) are arresting suspects in Berlin.

A change of mind

Odette did not want to leave her children. But Germany had occupied part of France in 1940, and many people, including her own family, were suffering as a result. So she decided to go. In October 1942, she landed in France and went to a safe house in Cannes. There she met Peter Churchill, the head of the local resistance.

Communications courier

Odette worked as a courier for the resistance, carrying communications between England and resistance groups in France. In 1943 Peter Churchill was ordered back to London. While waiting for his plane, both agents were nearly caught by the Germans. They escaped, but had to move their activities north, to the mountains of the Haute-Savoie.

Members of the French Resistance use a machine gun to fire on German troops in the streets of Paris.

Life in Ravensbrück

In May 1944, Odette was moved to Karlsruhe prison in Germany, and from there to the infamous Ravensbrück concentration camp.
At first, she was kept in an underground room in complete darkness, with only a plank to sleep on. Then she was moved to a tiny cell, where she remained in isolation until the Allies liberated the camp in May 1945. Odette had been kept apart from people for over a year. But she never broke under the pressure or gave the Germans the secret information they wanted.

Betrayal and capture

Odette and Peter started to work for the local resistance movement in their new area, but they were betrayed by a **double agent**. They were captured by the Gestapo and sentenced to death. To save Peter, Odette said that they were married and that she had forced him to come to France. She also claimed, more dangerously, to be a relative of the British prime minister, Winston Churchill. These lies may have prevented the two agents from being executed, but Odette was still tortured by the Gestapo. She refused to betray any of her resistance colleagues.

Odette and her future husband, Peter Churchill, shortly before their marriage in 1947.

Ravensbrück concentration camp

Ravensbrück concentration camp for women was built 50 miles (80 km) north of Berlin, the German capital. It was set up in 1938 to hold 6,000 inmates, but by the end of World War II, it housed more than 36,000.

From 1938 to 1945, over 50,000 women died in Ravensbrück, mostly as a result of harsh living conditions and hard labor. Some inmates were also injected with bacteria as part of a program of medical experiments. They often died or became disabled.

Sketches depicting life in the camp survive today. They show some of the terrible things the inmates had to endure.

After the war

When the war was over, Odette was awarded the George Cross for her bravery, the highest award that a civilian, or one who is not in the military, can be granted in Great Britain. She became famous when books and a film celebrating her wartime activities were produced.

Odette's first husband had died during the war, so she married Peter Churchill. But the couple's peacetime marriage was not a success, and they soon divorced. In 1956 Odette married a third time, to Geoffrey Hallowes.

Many ordinary people risked their lives in the resistance movements of occupied Europe. Some, like Odette Churchill, were brutally tortured by the enemy and yet never wavered in the fight for freedom.

RAOUL WALLENBERG

1912–?

The most appalling act to be carried out in World War II (1939–1945) was the mass murder of Jews by the Nazis. This later became known as the Holocaust. Raoul Wallenberg was brave enough to help some Jews escape their terrible fate.

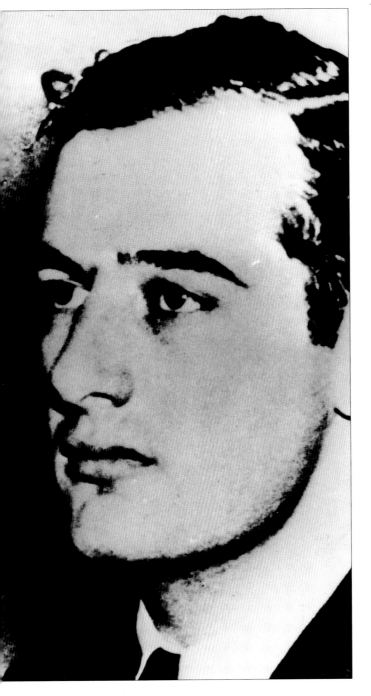

Wallenberg was born in Kappsta, near Stockholm, Sweden, in 1912. His family were rich **Lutherans**. As a young man, he studied architecture, then in 1936 became the foreign representative of a Central European trading company. Its president was a Hungarian Jew. Wallenberg worked hard for the company, and in 1939 made many business trips to Germany, France, and Hungary. He was a respected figure, especially in Budapest, Hungary's capital.

Nazi invasion

In March 1944, the Nazis sent troops into Hungary. The Germans had invaded mainly because they wanted to take the 700,000 Jews living there to concentration camps. Wallenberg was trusted by the Jewish community. So the Swedish and American governments, along with Jewish groups, such as the World Jewish Congress and the American War Refugee Board, persuaded him to work undercover in order to save some of the Hungarian Jews.

Raoul Wallenberg, a Swedish businessman whose bravery saved up to 100,000 Jews.

Adolf Eichmann

Adolf Eichmann joined the Nazi party as a young man and in 1942 was made responsible for the "Final Solution." This was the Nazi term for the mass execution of all European Jews. As a result of his plans, many Jews died in concentration camps (above). At the end of World War II in 1945, Eichmann escaped to Argentina. In 1958 Israel's secret agents arrested him. He was put on trial, found guilty, and hanged on May 31, 1962.

Rescue plans

Wallenberg's plan was to issue Jews with Swedish passports and to shelter them in protected houses, which flew the Swedish flag. Because Sweden was **neutral** during the war, the Germans could not act against it. Wallenberg operated from the Swedish embassy in Budapest, with a staff that grew from 20 to over 600 by the end of the war.

Saving the Jews

Through secret meetings with officials, and by using bribes and threats, Wallenberg managed to save up to 100,000 Jews. He also went to stations where Jews were being deported and distributed food and clothing. Other Jews were given money and official papers so that they could leave.

German troops deport a crowd of Hungarian Jews from the city of Budapest in 1944.

The Russian assault on Budapest in early 1945. Shortly afterward, Wallenberg was taken prisoner.

Heroic work

Wallenberg's heroic undercover work on behalf of the Jews, especially those living in the Budapest **ghetto**, earned him an international reputation. He was often threatened by the Nazis. But because Wallenberg was a citizen of a neutral country, they did not dare to interfere.

Arrest by the Soviets

Wallenberg's work was brought to a tragic end not by the Nazis, but by the Soviets. In January 1945, Soviet troops entered Budapest to liberate the city, and Wallenberg asked them to support his rescue missions. But his papers, radio, and unusual activities made the Soviets think that he was an American spy. They arrested him, then took him to Soviet headquarters. He never returned.

This is the last known photograph of Wallenberg. He sent it to his mother on November 26, 1944.

A great mystery

The mystery of Raoul Wallenberg started to grow. The Swedish authorities claimed that the Soviets had admitted his arrest was a mistake during a confused period at the end of the war, and that he had died of a heart attack in Moscow's Lubyanka Prison in 1947. But there were other, unconfirmed reports that Wallenberg had been seen alive in prison in 1951, 1959, and 1975.

Honorary citizen

On September 22, 1981, the United States granted Raoul Wallenberg honorary citizenship. Israel granted him the same honor in 1986, and a tree was planted there in his memory (see below). Tragically, we may never know what really happened to Wallenberg. But many thousands of people owe him their lives, and he was certainly one of the bravest undercover agents of all time.

Yad Vashem

Yad Vashem is Hebrew for "lasting memorial." This is the name of the monument established in Jerusalem in 1953 to preserve the memory of the Jews exterminated by Nazi Germany. The road leading up to it is known as the Avenue of the Righteous, and trees are planted there to commemorate non-Jews who risked their lives to save Jews. In 1986 a tree to honor Wallenberg was planted there (right).

GLOSSARY

Allies The countries that fought Germany together in World War II.

Appeasement The 1930s policy of keeping the peace with Germany by giving in to some of its demands.

Austro-Hungarian Empire The empire of Austria and the kingdom of Hungary combined. It lasted from 1867 to 1918.

Bavaria A former state, today an administrative region, in south Germany.

Blockade A ring of troops around a city.

British Expeditionary Force The first British troops sent to mainland Europe during World War II.

Chandler One who makes and sells candles.

Chief of staff The senior officer of each of the armed forces.

Cold War The political conflict between the United States and the Soviet Union during the 1950s and 1960s.

Communist A supporter of Communism, which states that all people are equal and property should not be privately owned.

Concentration camp A place in which large numbers of people are held by force and often inhumanely treated.

Constitution The laws according to which a country is governed.

Cossack A member of a people from southeast Russia who served as cavalry soldiers during times of war.

Cotton gin A machine that separates the seeds of cotton from the fibers.

Court-martial A military court where offenses against military law are tried.

Creditor A person, group, or country to whom money is owed.

Custody The right to care for and take charge of a child in one's home.

Deport To force someone to leave.

Divine right The belief that a monarch's right to rule comes from a supreme being.

Double agent A person who spies for two opposing powers at the same time.

Draft To select for military service during times of war.

Druggist One who owns a drugstore.

Federation A group of states that act separately on internal issues, but act together on foreign policy.

French and Indian War (1754–1763) A war between France and Great Britain that was fought in North America.

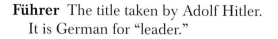

Führer The title taken by Adolf Hitler. It is German for "leader."

Ghetto An area in a town where one group of people lives apart from others.

Guerrilla A fighter who wages war by ambush and surprise attack.

Hanged, drawn, and quartered Hanged, cut open to remove the intestines, then chopped into pieces.

Hosiery Knitted stockings and socks.

Idol A statue worshiped as a god.

Intelligence Agency that obtains secret information.

Libel Publication of a statement that damages the reputation of a person or organization.

Lonely hearts Unattached people who advertise for a marriage partner.

Lutheran A person who believes in the religious doctrines of Martin Luther.

Military honors Signs of respect displayed by troops, such as saluting.

Militia A private army.

Nazi A follower of the German National Socialist movement led by Adolf Hitler.

Neutral Not allied to either side in a war.

Pillory A wooden frame with holes, in which a criminal's head and hands are locked.

Premier Prime minister.

Protestant A follower of the branch of Christianity that broke away from Roman Catholicism.

Rack An instrument of torture that stretches the body, causing extreme pain.

Reformation The sixteenth-century European movement that aimed to reform the Roman Catholic Church.

Resistance An organization working against an occupying army.

Roman Catholic A member of the Roman Catholic Church, which is led by the Pope in Rome, Italy.

Slav A member of a group of peoples living in Eastern Europe that includes Russians, Poles, and the peoples of the former Yugoslavia among others.

Subversion Activities designed to overthrow governments.

Telegraph An instrument that transmits electrical impulses along wires as a means of sending messages.

Yeomen of the Guard Soldiers who act as the British monarch's bodyguards.

INDEX